THE HERITAGE COLLECTION

RULERS and WARRIORESSES

Protectors of Dahomey

Letitia deGraft Okyere

Illustrated by Masum Ahmed

Rulers and Warrioresses: Protectors of Dahomey

Copyright © 2022 by Letitia deGraft Okyere

Illustrator: Masum Ahmed

Layout designer: Nasim Malik Sarkar

Library of Congress Control Number: 2022915390

All rights reserved.

No part of this publication may be reproduced, stored in a retrieval system, a database, and/or published in any form or by any means, electronic, mechanical, photocopying, recording or otherwise, without the prior written permission of the publisher.

ISBN 978-1-956776-11-9: hardback

ISBN 978-1-956776-12-6: ebook

Published by Lion's Historian Press

https://www.lionshistorian.net/

For

Gerard and Lily Anne

A Brief Introduction

In the early 1600s, the Kingdom of Dahomey in West Africa began to grow from the city-state called Abomey, occupied by the Fon-speaking people. Abomey started gaining influence in the region, during the reign of its first principal monarch, King Houegbadja. The Fon people then took the name Dahomey, with Abomey as its capital.

Dahomey expanded to include the neighboring kingdoms of Allada and Whydah. By the late 1700s, the Kingdom of Dahomey was well known for its regiment of fierce warrioresses, the *agoji*. They guarded the king (or queen), protected royal palaces, and defended the kingdom. European visitors named them the Dahomey Amazons in comparison to the Amazons of Greek mythology. The Greek Amazons were warrior women with courage, skill, and dedication, and lived in modern-day Ukraine, in Eastern Europe. The agoji, like their Greek counterparts, were fearless. The agoji sparked terror in Europeans and Dahomey's neighbors alike.

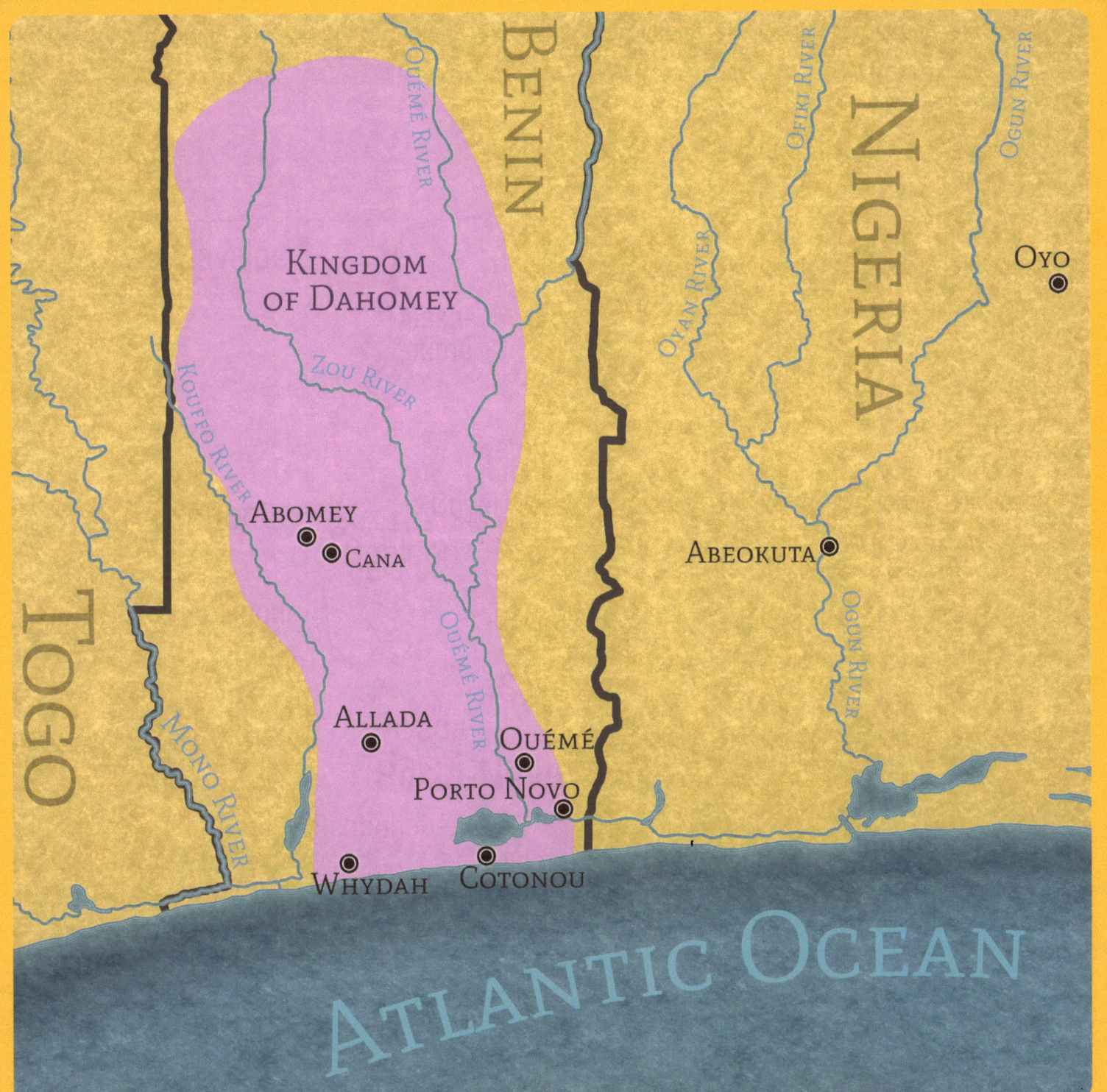

Contents

Chapter 1: The Foundation for Dahomey 1

Chapter 2: King Houegbadja's Reign 3

Chapter 3: The Rise of the Gbeto 5

Chapter 4: Early Appearance of the Agoji 7

Chapter 5: Queen Hangbé's Female Guards 9

Chapter 6: Increasing Military Strength 11

Chapter 7: The Oyo Victory and Egba Defeat 13

Chapter 8: Reorganization of the Agoji 15

Chapter 9: The Life of the Agoji 17

Chapter 10: King Ghezo and the Agoji 21

Chapter 11: The First Franco-Dahomean War 23

Chapter 12: The Second Franco-Dahomean War 27

Epilogue: The Kingdom Ends 31

Glossary 35

Quiz 37

References 38

Fun Fact About the Republic of Benin 40

Other Books in the Heritage Collection 41

CHAPTER 1

The Foundation for Dahomey

King Houegbadja is considered the first monarch of Dahomey. King Houegbadja's grandfather, Chief Do Aklin, led a group of people from Allada, another state in the region, near present-day Cotonou. The group traveled northwest to Houawé, on the Zou plateau, where they settled and mixed with the Fon-speaking people who lived there.

Houegbadja was young when his grandfather Do Aklin died, and his uncle Dako became king. Dako overcame resistance from local chiefs and strengthened his authority in the area. An older Houegbadja rose to fame by bravely defeating one of two chiefs who continued to threaten King Dako's reign.

After Houegbadja's victory, King Dako refused to give him the honor due, fearing competition. Instead, Dako suggested that Houegbadja create a new city in neighboring Abomey, ruled by the wicked Chief Dan, the second of the two chiefs. Houegbadja accepted the challenge knowing his uncle expected him to fail. Houegbadja went bearing gifts to Chief Dan, seeking permission before he settled at Abomey around 1625. Houegbadja showed that he was not only brave but wise.

King Houegbadja's Reign

Houegbadja's status grew because he conquered neighboring hostile chiefs. This made Chief Dan jealous, and he plotted Houegbadja's death, but his attempts failed. When Chief Dan was killed during a conflict, it made way for the new kingdom called Dahomey, meaning *out of the belly of Dan*. Chief Dan, annoyed by Houegbadja's expanding borders, made fun of the settlers, asking if they wanted to build houses in his belly. After Chief Dan's death, Abomey became Dahomey's capital.

Most importantly, King Houegbadja laid the foundation for the role of women as protectors of the kingdom. He established the corps of elephant huntresses. Also, with his primary wife, Nanye Adonon, King Houegbadja had twins, a son called Akaba, and a daughter, Tassi Hangbé. Twins were considered special in the kingdom, and it led to the principle of *dualism*, where all male officials had a female counterpart who lived at the palace. They believed that dualism was necessary for completeness. Even the king had a counterpart known as the *kpodjito*, or queen mother. Royal protocol gave priority to women officials over their male counterparts.

King Houegbadja's reign was successful in other ways. He created a constitution, royal council, and system of taxes, and passed laws governing kingdom operations. King Houegbadja appointed ministers and administrators. The grand palace that he built was extended by each successor king, becoming home to thousands of royal household members. Houegbadja reigned for forty years following Dako's death in Houawé.

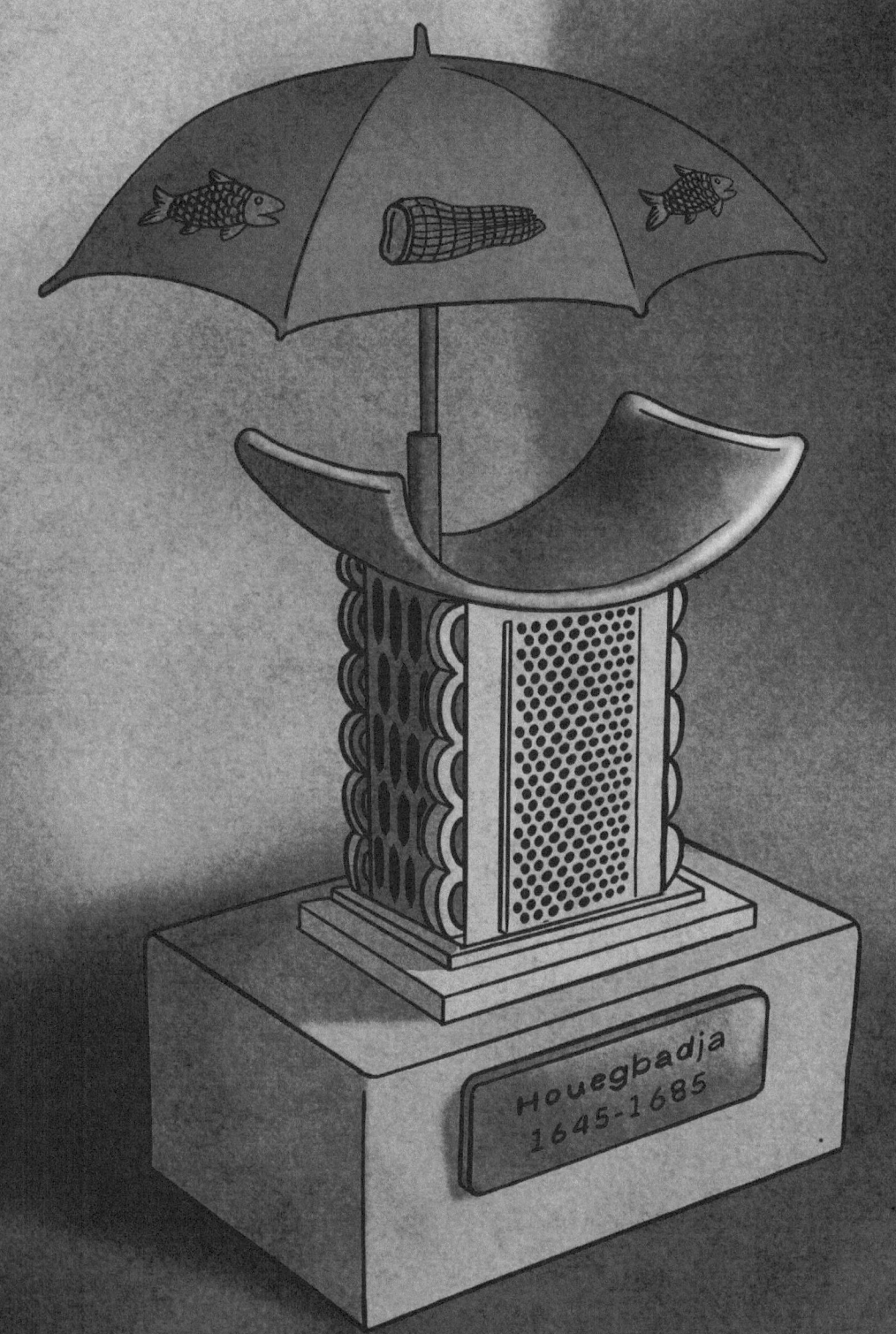

CHAPTER 3

The Rise of the Gbeto

King Houegbadja's special corps of elephant huntresses, known as the *gbeto*, supplied ivory for trade and meat for palace tables. Historians write that the gbeto was the early start to the elite warrioresses. Not just any female could join the gbeto. Palace officials traveled across the kingdom, looking for young girls with the right physical appearance and character, and the king selected the final group of trainees. The gbeto consisted of strong and determined women, as elephant hunting was dangerous and difficult.

When the gbeto completed a hunt, they attended the king's court for awards with elephant tails, their victory trophies. The gbeto appeared chanting conquest songs that described how they hunted. They formed circles and crawled on their knees toward elephants, with hunting guns in hand. The gbeto could get close because elephants were deceived by the antelope horns, worn as crowns.

By the 1800s, the gbeto's uniform consisted of brown skirts with blue tops reaching down to the mid-thigh, secured with a black sash. The skirt's front was decorated with cowries, polished shells of sea snails. On the back were strips of dried animal skin covered with black animal hair, tied to the black sash. They wore their hair cut low, covered with two antelope horns. The gbeto was an important part of Dahomean society. They participated in city square royal parades, where they displayed hunting tools and skills with song and dance. In later years, the gbeto joined the warrioresses on war expeditions.

CHAPTER 4

Early Appearance of the Agoji

Akaba became king after his father Houegbadja's death in 1685, and the role of women in the kingdom increased. King Akaba reigned jointly with his twin sister, Tassi Hangbé. Though she was largely a silent partner, she had a military role. King Akaba created a special unit of male warriors for his sister, known as the *Company of Queen Hangbé*.

King Akaba used women as law enforcers. As many as three hundred went to villages carrying sticks to settle disputes, with the ability to punish for disobedience. As the women's policing and combat functions increased, their fame as warrioresses began to grow. The warrioresses, known as the agoji, would participate in battles. These women were Dahomean or from conquered states.

Akaba, with his sister's support, decided to expand eastward. King Akaba conquered a Yoruba group of people. Next, in 1708, he turned his attention to Ouémé, led by King Yahazé, on the Ouémé River. The agoji supported King Akaba, fighting the enemy with swords. Agoji songs tell of King Yahazé's defeat and how they positioned themselves in the shallow parts of the Ouémé River like mangrove trees. The warrioresses were trained to help enlarge the kingdom's border and provide conquests.

CHAPTER 5

Queen Hangbé's Female Guards

Tassi Hangbé became queen in 1708. European traders who had landed at the Port of Whydah brought smallpox, and it spread quickly among native populations. King Akaba caught smallpox and died during the war with Ouémé; Hangbé agreed to continue the conflict as the commander-in-chief. She posed as her twin brother on the war front until victory. The royal council then decided to appoint her queen regent, as Akaba's heir was too young to rule.

Queen Hangbé built a group of female palace guards to protect her. They accompanied her on trips beyond palace gates and performed at customary ceremonies. They traveled with her when she went to war. A young Princess Hangbé had been interested in the adventures of the elephant huntresses. Zognidi was a senior gbeto who presented hunt trophies at King Houegbadja's court. After Zognidi's meetings, she often stepped out to find Princess Hangbé waiting with questions. Queen Hangbé had created her corps of palace guards with members of gbeto teams.

Queen Hangbé's courage to engage in expansion wars was likely tied to the lessons learned from Zognidi's hunting adventures. Queen Hangbé's reign lasted three years, during which she won two additional military campaigns. It is believed that the agoji provided support when Hangbé went to war. During Hangbé's reign, not only did dualism allow for women administrators at the palace, but also, women increasingly took on combat roles as huntresses, enforcers, palace guards, and warrioresses.

Chapter 6

Increasing Military Strength

Agadja, the younger brother of Akaba and Hangbé, took over in 1711. King Agadja built a disciplined army that was kept standing and encamped wherever the king lodged, unusual in that part of Africa at the time. In addition to the female warrior units, there was also the corps of female palace guards. They continued as gatekeepers because men could not be at the palace after dark. The female palace guards acted as bodyguards for the king and members of the royal household.

King Agadja planned to increase the kingdom's wealth through direct access to European trade at the ports. In 1724, he traveled south, conquered his ancestral home of Allada, and moved to the Port of Whydah. After several failed attempts, Agadja offered his daughter to Whydah's king in marriage. Naturally, the princess would have to settle in Whydah with servants. Agadja and troops camped by Whydah's capital identified its gun powder depot. At Agadja's instruction, warrioresses disguised as the princess' assistants poured water on the supply as other female units entered the city, defeating Whydah in 1729.

With his stronger army, Agadja prevented raids where the Fon people were taken captive and sold. However, through his southern conquests, Agadja officially commenced trading with the Europeans. This sadly meant that Dahomey participated in the trans-Atlantic slave trade until decades later, when British blockades took effect. European traders noticed the use of skilled and armed females to protect the kingdom. Palace guests at Abomey found armed women on guard at entrances, while female guards and warrioresses surrounded the king at his court.

CHAPTER 7

The Oyo Victory and Egba Defeat

In 1818, King Ghezo, Agadja's great-grandson, became king. Ghezo planned to free Dahomey from the tax imposed by the eastern Oyo Empire. When King Agadja failed to defeat the Oyo during his war with them, the Oyo imposed a tax on Dahomey. It was a heavy burden, requiring forty-one of many items, such as muskets, barrels of gun powder, strings of beads, as well as men and women to work in Oyo as servants. In Dahomey, forty-one was the number for royal excellence, and only kings could present a gift of this number.

When the King of Oyo sent his representative for his yearly tribute, King Ghezo declared war. Ghezo marched with his army, including the feared agoji. The warrioresses distinguished themselves during the war, taking down Oyo defenses and ending the requirement for the tribute around 1823. Afterward, Ghezo expanded the kingdom through successful military campaigns, with the warrioresses as a regular part of his army.

In 1844, King Ghezo's troops suffered a shocking defeat. The Egbas of Abeokuta, from about one hundred miles east of Abomey, launched a surprise attack. Many of Ghezo's troops died, including his prized warrioresses. King Ghezo vowed revenge, particularly as the loss affected the reputation of his warrioresses. King Ghezo decided to reorganize the agoji.

CHAPTER 8

Reorganization of the Agoji

King Ghezo began a recruitment process increasing the force's size to thousands. A national census was used to track estimates of females in each family, then the king's representatives visited provinces to see if these young girls would be suitable for royal service. Sometimes, wealthy families offered daughters in exchange for influence at the palace. Other times, badly behaved daughters were sent to the palace for discipline. Ghezo included captives because he believed they made the most loyal subjects; they owed him their lives, freedom, and privileged social position.

The recruits had a difficult training program. It started early at dawn and continued late into the day. They practiced hand-to-hand combat, the use of new European arms, and physical training to improve speed and strength. Trainees walked and ran for long distances; the fastest were assigned to the musket unit, and the slower ones became archers. They had survival exercises where they lived in the bush for nine days with few supplies. They entered mock fortified cities by climbing barricades made from thorny acacia bushes. At night, they trained through wrestling matches or repaired the thorny obstacles.

King Ghezo created a professional army comparable to the European armies he had seen. The agoji was commanded by female officers of equal rank as their male counterparts. Ghezo built an elite force of women skilled in handling swords, rifles, spears, and other European weapons. However, they rarely used shields and did not ride horses or other animals.

CHAPTER 9

The Life of the Agoji

The warrioresses belonged to a special class with many privileges. They were the king's wives, or *ahosi*. The ahosi was made up of three groups. The king lived with the first two groups as partners and had children with them. The third group was the warrioresses, classed as wives because they belonged to the king. They were not allowed to get married or have children.

The agoji lived at the king's palaces and had all their needs met. Each warrioress had about fifty servants to cook and clean for her, even going with the warrioress on military campaigns. When an agoji traveled outside the palace, a little servant girl walked before her, ringing a bell, warning people of a warrioress' appearance. The public had to move or look away.

The warrioresses were unusual in the region because they had uniforms for battle and parades. Battle dresses tended to be brown or grey, and those for parades were brightly colored, made from fine fabrics. Each unit had its own flags and banners and specially decorated umbrellas for officers. Common unit symbols were alligators, red sharks, or red zigzag patterns. They also wore white skull caps with their unit's symbol on the front. During drills and military parades, they danced to music and song.

Rumors of the fierce-looking corps of female defenders traveled far and near, instilling fear in both European and African opponents. Guests to King Ghezo's court found a display of his elite female defenders in perfect stillness. On the king's right were six hundred female palace guards, squatting on rugs

with guns between their legs; behind them was a line of elephant huntresses, dressed in brown uniforms with their hunting rifles. On the king's left were about two hundred female government administrators. Standing behind the king were four agoji and the agoji general-in-chief. The king's heir and principal ministers were positioned on the steps before the king.

CHAPTER 10

King Ghezo and the Agoji

King Ghezo's reorganization also extended to government systems, as the slave trade had ended. Ghezo invested in trade and diplomatic relations with Europeans and created a centralized tax system. The kingdom moved to large-scale production of palm oil, required by Europeans for their factories. Following Ghezo's reorganization of government systems, including the army, he turned his attention to plans to extend Dahomey's borders.

King Ghezo and his male troops attacked a commercial center located some sixty miles northwest of Abomey. When the inhabitants of the city heard of the Dahomean approach, all fled except the soldiers. The city's soldiers held back the Dahomean troops, killing many. King Ghezo realized that they might be defeated, and he sent for his warrioresses. They moved with speed, defeating the resisting soldiers and saving Dahomey from destruction. The agoji also defeated the Ado in the east, who had contributed to Ghezo's defeat by the Egbas. The agoji marched past the Ado city and then doubled back at night.

Dahomey's battle victories led to attacks on its neighboring villages and towns by people from the east, the Yorubas. King Ghezo decided it was time to conquer the Egbas of Abeokuta in 1851. Ghezo's six thousand female troops were led by his young commander, Sehdong. However, Ghezo made two mistakes. He sent a message of his impending invasion through visiting Europeans and took strategic advice from a chief sympathetic to the Egbas. The agoji tasted defeat again. Ghezo conducted other campaigns after this second Egba defeat but did not try to invade Abeokuta again.

CHAPTER 11

The First Franco-Dahomean War

King Béhanzin came to the throne as the nineteenth century grew to a close, when European powers busily acquired portions of Africa as colonies for access to rich natural resources. King Béhanzin was King Ghezo's grandson, and he vowed to retain control of his kingdom.

Dahomey claimed a small state in the south called Porto Novo, but it rejected Dahomey and sought French protection. Dahomey responded with military attacks to retain control. The French then built up its forces in Cotonou, even though this city was also claimed by Dahomey. The French insisted that Dahomey gave Cotonou away by a treaty in 1868 and 1878. King Béhanzin, on the other hand, disputed the content and purpose of these agreements. The French extended its authority in Cotonou, leading to conflicts. Later, the French arrested senior Dahomean officials.

Reports of these issues were relayed to King Béhanzin, and in March 1890, Dahomean forces marched to Cotonou. King Béhanzin argued that the French interfered with his rights in the region. The agoji worked on destroying the barricade installed by the French, pulling stakes apart and firing through. Other agoji, including Nansica, climbed over for hand-to-hand combat. Nansica was a young and beautiful agoji who fought intensely. She killed a French soldier operating a cannon from behind the barricade. Nansica saw how many of the warrioresses had been killed by this French soldier and sought revenge. At a later battle which Nansica did not live to see, the agoji pushed the French back into a retreat.

After suffering some losses, Dahomean forces regrouped, and with two thousand agoji, they headed towards Porto Novo. Native Porto Novo forces fled on the agoji's approach, leaving French troops who had stronger gunpowder. Despite this, the agoji forced the French into retreat beyond their barricades. The battle between the agoji and the French troops continued for several hours until the rains came, ending the war.

King Béhanzin ordered a return to Abomey, and he did not send any more troops to Porto Novo or Cotonou. The French sent a priest to negotiate a peace agreement. King Béhanzin gave up Cotonou and signed a treaty recognizing Porto Novo as a French territory.

CHAPTER 12

The Second Franco-Dahomean War

King Béhanzin remained unhappy with the French and continued to dispute their right to occupy Cotonou. Also, King Béhanzin recognized he was unevenly matched against the French in 1890 and purchased weapons from German traders. France sought opportunities to remove King Béhanzin. In March 1892, a French gunboat in Dahomean territory was shot at by King Béhanzin's troops, opening the door for conflict. France quickly raised a force of over three thousand heavily armed men. Next, France blocked Dahomey's access to the coast, preventing additional arms purchases, and started a march to Abomey.

Several battles during the march to Abomey inflicted heavy losses on the agoji because the French had more advanced weapons. However, the undeterred agoji launched fierce charges, also causing losses to France. When agoji numbers reduced, they turned to digging trenches and foxholes to slow down the French troops. The final battle at Cana, in early November of 1892, lasted a whole day, leading to the agoji's defeat. Even then, the agoji refused to give up. They dressed up as regular peasants in the evening and infiltrated the French camp, inflicting more losses.

King Béhanzin sent a peace mission before the French troops arrived in Abomey. When this failed, rather than allow his capital to fall into the hands of his enemy, he evacuated the city and set it on fire. King Béhanzin fled with his remaining army to the north while the French claimed victory. Dahomey became a part of France's colony in West Africa, called French Dahomey.

While in hiding, King Béhanzin tried to rebuild his army and corps of warrioresses, but the effort was unsuccessful. He surrendered in January 1894 and was exiled to Martinique. King Béhanzin left Martinique for Algeria a few years later, where he died and was buried. His remains were returned to French Dahomey in 1928.

EPILOGUE

The Kingdom Ends

In Dahomey, women played a significant role in shaping the country's history. The principle of dualism placed them in administrative positions of responsibility. In addition, women as defenders of Dahomey challenged traditional male perceptions that women did not engage in war. Dahomean women displayed determination and strength as members of the gbeto, palace guard, and agoji.

The agoji fought their last battle at Cana, home of the king's country palace, in November 1892. The warrioresses were described as fearless enemies even when defeat seemed likely. Some historians estimate that as many as fifteen thousand warrioresses lost their lives trying to protect the Kingdom of Dahomey during the last wars of the nineteenth century. The French praised the agoji as willing to safeguard Dahomey's interests, even if it meant the sacrifice of death. The agoji was more disciplined and skilled than their male counterparts.

In 1960, French Dahomey was declared independent as the Republic of Dahomey and later became the Republic of Benin. Many wondered if any warrioresses lived to witness this significant political change. They had finally attained freedom from French colonial masters. Almost twenty years later, there were reports of a woman called Nawi who lived at Kinta, a village thirty minutes south of Abomey. Nawi disclosed she had fought in the final war against the French in 1892, alongside King Béhanzin. Many were pleased with the discovery; at least one warrioress had lived to see her country free.

The Republic of Benin is located between West Africa's countries of Burkina Faso, Togo, Nigeria, and Niger. Remnants of Dahomey may be found in the southern part of present-day Benin. Abomey is the capital of Benin's Zou region, a tourist site, and a principal place for arts and crafts. Sections of the Royal Palaces of Abomey from 1600 to 1900, occupied by Dahomey's royalty and its women warriors, still exist today.

The history of the warrioresses is recorded in clay sculptures on the walls of Dahomey's palaces. They are also honored with song and dance in Benin. There is an old statue of a Dahomey warrioress in a village near Abomey. Recently in the Republic of Benin, a ninety-eight feet high bronze statue was unveiled in Cotonou, at the public square called *Esplanade des Amazones*, to ensure that the contribution of the warrioresses to the Kingdom of Dahomey is never forgotten. The agoji was the first known all female army in modern history.

Glossary

Kingdom of Dahomey — A kingdom in West Africa, now a part of the Republic of Benin. Benin's capital is Porto Novo, and its seat of government is in Cotonou.

Agoji — The famed female warriors of the Kingdom of Dahomey.

Abomey — Capital city of the Kingdom of Dahomey, now a tourist city in the Republic of Benin's Zou Department or region.

Whydah — Also written as Ouidah, was a small kingdom on the Atlantic coast conquered by the Kingdom of Dahomey. It is now a part of the Republic of Benin.

Allada — Allada, the ancestral home of Dahomey's monarchs, was a small kingdom in the same region as Abomey. It was later conquered by the Kingdom of Dahomey.

King Houegbadja	King Houegbadja is considered the first monarch of Dahomey. His name comes from *houé gb'adja, man yi adja*, meaning *the fish that escaped the trap does not return to it*. Houegbadja believed he had escaped King Dako's trap by refusing to return to Houawé despite Dako's offers. Thus, King Houegbadja adopted a fish and trap net as his emblem.
Gbeto	The corps of elephant huntresses in the Kingdom of Dahomey.
Ouémé River	The largest river in the Republic of Benin.
Oyo Empire	The Oyo Empire was a powerful state of the Yoruba people and the largest Yoruba-speaking nation. It was made up of modern-day eastern Benin and western Nigeria.
Ahosi	The king's wives. This group included the agoji.

Quiz

1. Who was the first King of Dahomey?

    (a) King Akaba
    (b) King Ghezo
    (c) King Houegbadja
    (d) King Agadja

2. Who were the royal twins?

    (a) Akaba and Agajda
    (b) Akaba and Tassi Hangbé
    (c) Agadja and Tassi Hangbé
    (d) Agadja and Ghezo

3. What was the name of the elite female corps of warriors?

    (a) Gbeto
    (b) Royal Palace Guards
    (c) The Company of Queen Hangbé
    (d) Agoji

4. What was the name of the last King of Dahomey, before the French took over?

    (a) Béhanzin
    (b) Glélé
    (c) Ghezo
    (d) Akaba

QUIZ ANSWERS: CBDA

References

Larsen, Lynne E. (2021). Wives and Warriors: The Royal Women of Dahomey as Representatives of the Kingdom. In *The Routledge Companion to Black Women's Cultural Histories*, chap. 22. Abingdon: Routledge, 2021. https://doi.org/10.4324/9780429243578.

Medali, Dallys-Tom. *Kings, Queens and Amazons of Dahomey*. Paris, Solara Editions, 2020.

Kaur, Mukhwinder. "Mother of Nations and Kali's Daughters: An Empirical Study on Amazon Dahomey Warriors and Indian Queen Warriors." *Military Science Review*, vol. 10, no. 4, 2017, pp. 126-141.

Kelly, Julia. "Dahomey! Dahomey!: The Reception of Dahomean Art in France in the late 19th and early 20th Centuries." *Journal of Art Historiography*, no. 12, 2015, pp. 1-19.

Alpern, Stanley B. *Amazons of Black Sparta: The Women Warriors of Dahomey*. New York, New York University Press, 2011.

Adams, Maeve E. "The Amazon Warrior Woman and the De/construction of Gendered Imperial Authority in Nineteenth-Century Colonial Literature." *Nineteenth-Century Gender Studies*, no. 6.1, 2010, pp. 24-40.

Holloway, Nada. (2009). Dahomey Women's Army. In I. Ness (Ed.), *The International Encyclopedia of Revolution and Protest*. Accessed July 12, 2022. https://doi.org/10.1002/9781405198073.wbierp0433.

Edgerton, Robert B. *Warrior Women: The Amazons of Dahomey and the Nature of War*. Boulder, Westview Press, 2000.

Alpern, Stanley B. "On the Origins of the Amazons of Dahomey." *History of Africa*, vol. 25, 1995, pp. 9-25.

Law, Robin. "The 'Amazons' of Dahomey." *Paideuma*, vol. 39, 1993, pp. 245-260.

Davidson, Basil. *A History of West Africa* 1000-1800. Singapore, Longman, 1977.

Fun Fact About the Republic of Benin

Lake Nokoué, which is in the southern part of the country and borders the city of Cotonou, is home to the "Venice of Africa." The natives built Ganvié village in the middle of Lake Nokoué, four hundred years ago, to avoid being captured and sold to European traders. Local soldiers who conducted raids were afraid of the lake because they believed it had evil spirits. After the slave trade ended, the native people continued to build homes in the lake even though the threat was gone. Today, the village has about thirty thousand people, and all buildings — homes, schools, markets, beauty salons — rest on stilts.

Other Books in the Heritage Collection

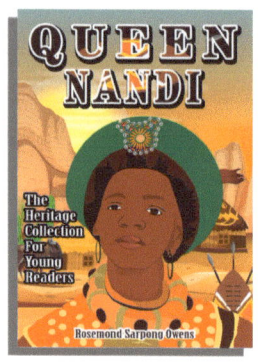

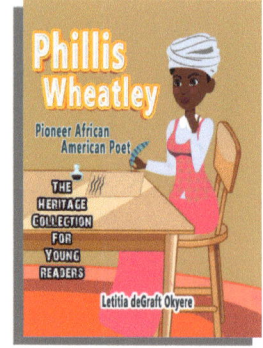
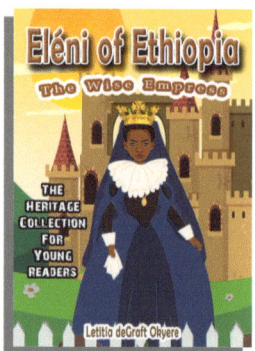
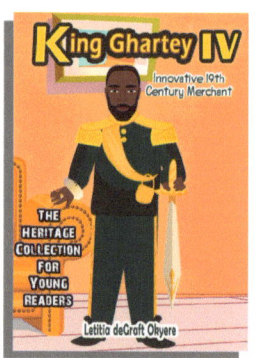
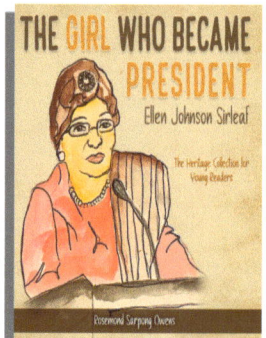
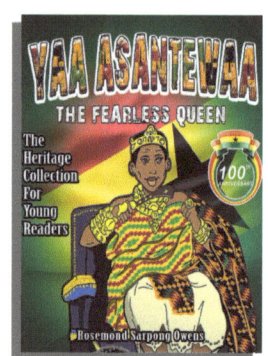
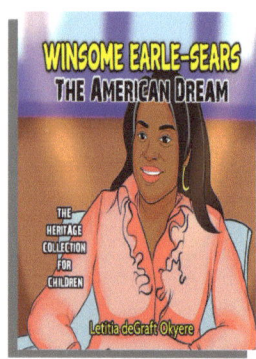
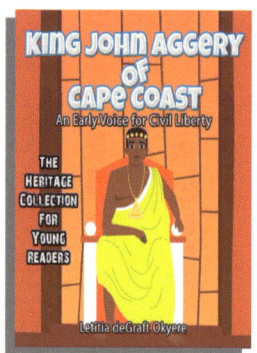

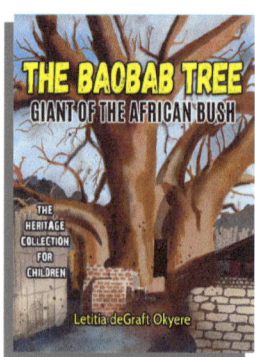

www.ingramcontent.com/pod-product-compliance
Lightning Source LLC
Chambersburg PA
CBHW041407010526
44107CB00015B/1097